Sch

D0306331

I CAN HELP
Recycle Rubbish

Viv Smith

W
FRANKLIN WATTS
LONDON • SYDNEY

First Published in 1998 by
Franklin Watts

Franklin Watts
96 Leonard Street
London EC2A 4XD

Franklin Watts Australia
56 O'Riordan Street
Alexandria, Sydney
NSW 2015

Editor: Helen Lanz
Art Director: Robert Walster
Designer: Sally Boothroyd
Environmental consultant: John Baines
Commissioned photography: Steve Shott
Illustrations: Kim Woolley

ISBN: 0 7496 4292 0

Dewey Decimal Number: 363.72
A CIP catalogue record for this book is available from the British Library.

Printed in Hong Kong

Picture Credits
Cover: Steve Shott
Interior pictures: Franklin Watts/Chris Honeywell 12 tr & 24 t; Harry Cory-Wright 18 tl; Oxfam/Crispin Hughes 22 b; Viv Smith 8 tr & br; Still Pictures 12 b. All other interior photographs by Steve Shott.

The publishers would like to thank St Leonard's Primary School, Stafford, for their help and enthusiasm, especially Viv Smith and Class 2S who feature in this series.

Thank you also to Still Pictures for photographs supplied for this book.

Contents

A load of rubbish!

Rubbish is made up of the things we throw away when we no longer want them. We get rid of them by putting them in the bin. But do we really need to make so much waste?

Fascinating Fact!

In Britain we throw away about 20 million tonnes of rubbish a year – the same weight as 55 thousand jumbo-jets or 3 million elephants!

Have a Go!

Get everyone in your class to collect all the rubbish you and your families throw away in one day.

Would there be more rubbish if yesterday had been a special occasion – like Christmas Day or your birthday? Imagine how much bigger the pile would be after a week.

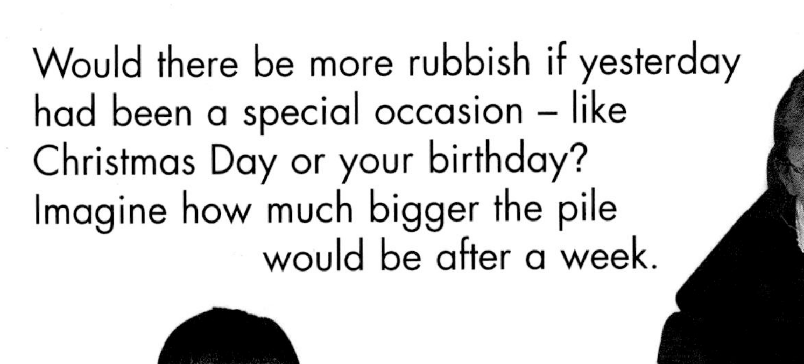

Watch Out!

Always wear rubber gloves if you touch rubbish. Ask an adult to help. Some of the rubbish will need washing before you take it to school. Put food scraps in a bag or container.

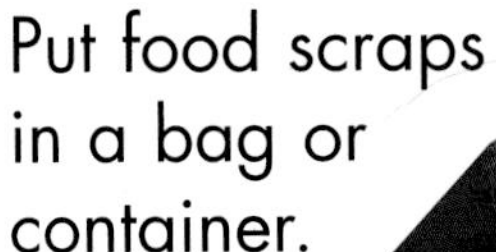

From the earth

Everything we use and throw away is made from the earth's natural resources. These are water, oil, coal, gas, air, rocks, plants and animals.

The paper that you write on was once a tree that stood in a forest. Your aluminium drink can was once rocks. Glass bottles were once sand. Material for clothes comes from plants, animals, or chemicals made from oil.

Trees in forests like this are cut down and taken to a paper mill (below). The wood is cut up and turned into a pulp to make paper.

Imagine you were given a huge jar of sweets but you could not have any more when they were gone.

Eat them slowly and carefully, and you can enjoy them for a long time. Gobble them all up at once and they will soon disappear.

Some of the earth's natural resources, such as oil, coal and gas, are like this. They will disappear if we do not use them carefully.

FASCINATING FACT!

Some natural resources, such as trees, can be replaced, but we must not use them faster than new ones can grow.

FASCINATING FACT!

If we use oil and gas in the same way and in the same amounts as we do today, they will be in very short supply in the next 80 years or so.

We need to use the earth's resources sensibly so there are enough left for the people who come after us.

What is rubbish made of?

Have you ever looked to see exactly what is in the bin?

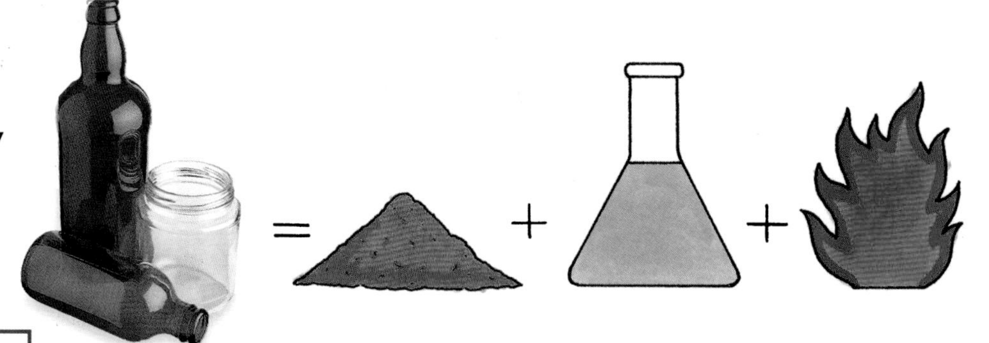

Glass is made from a mixture of sand, chemicals and limestone. (Limestone is a rock.) All these ingredients are heated up to make glass.

HAVE A GO!

Sort through what has been thrown away. Put the rubbish into different groups.

GLASS
METAL
PAPER AND CARDBOARD
CLOTH
PLASTIC
FOOD

Do you know what these groups of rubbish are made from?

Most metals are found in rocks in the ground. The rocks are crushed and heated. The metal in the rocks melts and is collected.

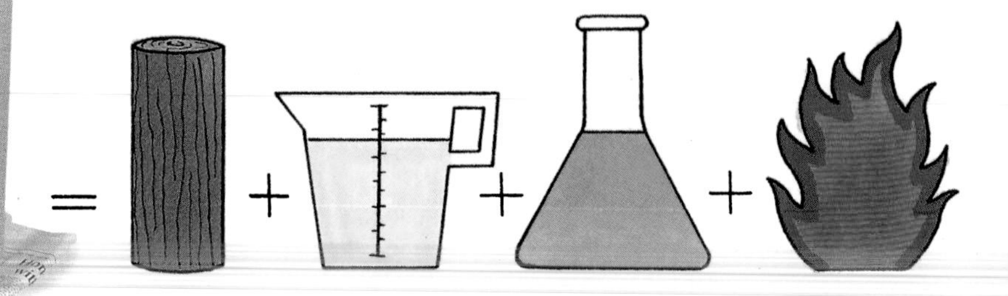

Wood, cut into tiny pieces, is mixed with water and chemicals to make paper. Today, many trees are specially planted and grown for making paper.

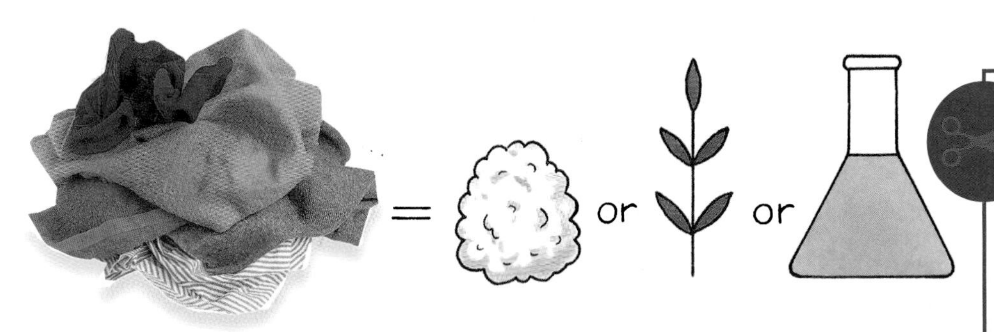

Some materials, like wool, come from animals. Cotton comes from plants. These are natural materials. Other materials are made from chemicals that are not found naturally. But these chemicals come from natural resources, such as oil.

Plastic is not a natural material. But it is made from natural resources: oil, gas and coal.

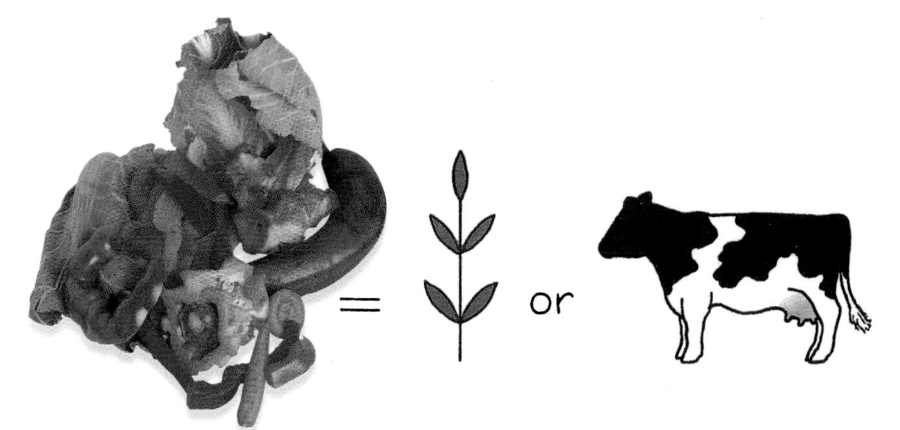

All plants need water, warm sunshine and food from the soil to grow. All animals depend on the earth for their food. In turn, they provide us with food.

HAVE A GO!

Choose one of the groups of rubbish from these pages. Design a poster to show what the rubbish is made of.

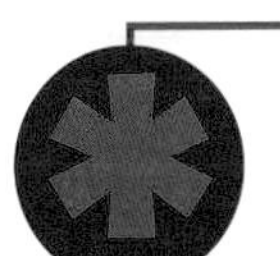

WATCH OUT!

Remember the warning on page 7 about touching rubbish.

The problem with rubbish

Have you ever thought about what happens to your rubbish?

Your bin is emptied into a refuse-collecting lorry. The rubbish is taken to a huge hole in the ground where it is buried. This is a landfill site (below). Some rubbish is burnt in an incinerator.

Our rubbish is usually collected from outside our homes once a week.

Rubbish in the wrong place is litter. Litter, such as broken bottles or plastic bags, can harm people and wildlife.

Fascinating Fact!

A box of chocolates may have more than 6 layers of packaging. But the same chocolates can sometimes be bought in just one bag. They taste just as good and produce far less rubbish.

Getting rid of rubbish can be a problem. Burning it can make the air dirty. Rotting rubbish in landfill sites produces an explosive gas which has to be controlled. We need to make sure that the rubbish we throw away cannot pollute the ground or our water supplies.

The world is running out of places where rubbish can be dumped.

Fascinating Facts!

Re-use your plastic shopping bag as many times as you can. Plastic bags can be very wasteful because they don't rot. They simply fill up space in the landfill site.

Re-using and recycling

Many of the things we put into the bin can be re-used. 'Re-using' means to use something again. Empty washing powder containers can be refilled. Good clothes can be given to someone else when you have grown out of them.

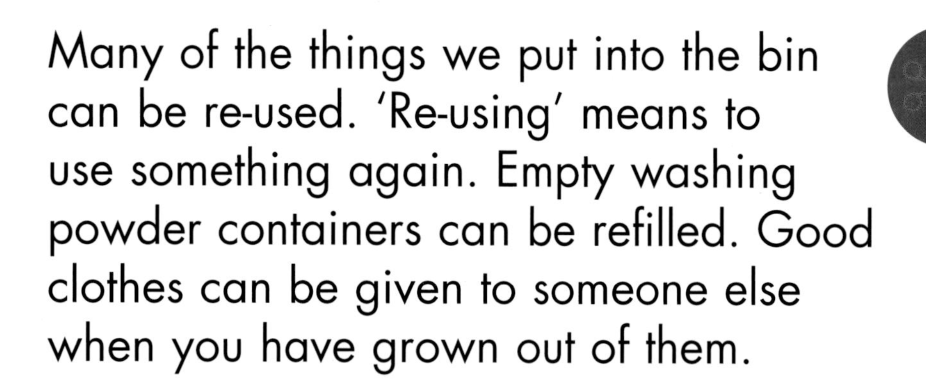

HAVE A GO!

Next time you go out shopping, make a list of all the containers that could be refilled or used again.

We already re-use some things without even thinking about it – does your family have a second-hand car?

Here, old newspaper is being re-used. It is being torn up to make a papier mâché model.

To 'recycle' means to make something new out of something that has been used before.

Paper can be recycled. If water is added to waste paper it makes a pulp. This is like the pulp made from wood (see pages 8 and 10). It can be used to make recycled paper.

All these things have been made from recycled paper. When you go shopping, see if you can see any other goods made of recycled paper.

HAVE A GO!

Ask if you can have a paper recycling bank at your school. Make a poster to tell everyone where it is and what to put in it.

FASCINATING FACT!

Nearly half the paper used to make newspapers in Britain has been recycled.

A swappers' club

Making things uses up a lot of energy and natural resources. We can help by re-using and recycling things. This reduces, or uses less, of these resources. The more things we swap and re-use, the fewer new things need to be made.

Why not start a Swappers' Club at school? Exchange unwanted things.

Have a Go!

Ask your teacher, or another adult, to help you run a competition for the best item made out of waste. Give prizes for the funniest ideas as well as the best.

Have a Go!

Make a list of all the things you think your classmates might re-use. Ask them, and tick off what they actually have re-used. Are there any things that you didn't think of?

yogurt carton
ice cream tub
toilet roll tube
washing up bottle
shoe box
string
milk bottle tops
rubber ban

Fascinating Fact!

In Britain, over three-quarters of the rubbish thrown away could be re-used or recycled.

Look Back

Can you see things in the rubbish piles on pages 6 and 7 which could have been re-used?

Going shopping

When you go shopping, encourage your family and friends to buy things which are made from recycled materials or which can be recycled themselves.

Keep a look out for different recycling signs when you visit the shops. Why do you think the arrows of the sign on the left are going round and round?

HAVE A GO!

Check the prices of recycled goods. Compare them with the same items which are not made from recycled materials. Are they more expensive?

If we buy more recycled things, more of them will be made. If more are made they will become cheaper.

Don't forget to look for the recycling signs.

HAVE A GO!

Make a shopping bag which can be used over and over again. Find some strong scrap fabric. Get an adult to help you cut it out and sew it. Decorate it with a picture or a message which will tell everyone that the owner of the bag is a recycling fan.

You will need:

2 large rectangles of material for the front and back
2 thin strips of material for the handles
needle and thread
fabric paint and a paint brush
pencil and scissors

1. Ask an adult to help you cut out the 4 pieces of material
2. With help from your teacher, mum or dad, sew along one long edge of the large rectangles, along the bottom edge and up the other long side. Make sure you leave the top free so you can put your shopping in!
3. Sew the handles onto the bag. Make sure they are on firmly.
4. Draw your recycling sign onto your bag with a pencil.
5. Use the fabric paint to colour the recycling sign.

Going to the bank

Do you know where your local recycling centre is? It could be closer than you think if you help set one up at school.

Have a Go!

Recipe for an aluminium recycling bank:
A group of children
Some helpful adults
A safe place to store squashed cans
People who will buy cans from you
Mix well.
Tell everyone what you are doing and why.

Ask your teacher to arrange for someone to take the cans to a place where they can be recycled. You can get information about this from your local Council Recycling Officer.

Get an adult to help you sort the cans. A magnet will be useful. Do you know why?

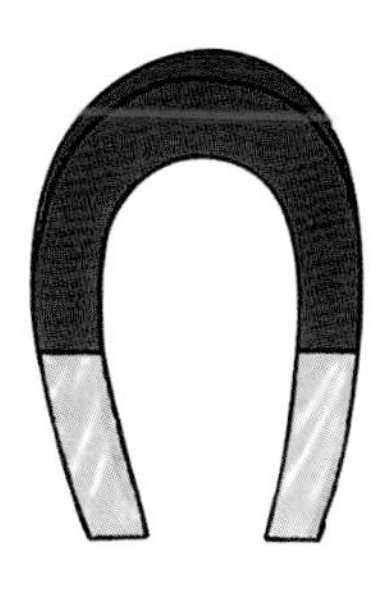

Answer: If the metal can is attracted to the magnet, it is not made of aluminium, so don't put it in the recycling bin.

Fascinating Fact!

It takes the same amount of energy to make 20 recycled aluminium cans as it does to make just one new can from aluminium ore.

Recycling in your area

Are there people in your local area who could use some of the things you throw away? What you can no longer use might be just what someone else is looking for.

HAVE A GO!

Surprise your family. Tidy out your room! Collect all the unwanted things that are cluttering up your cupboards. Take them to your local charity shop or to a jumble sale. Or how about a car-boot sale?

When you buy things from a charity shop, you are helping other people, as well as the environment.

You can help in your area by picking up litter where you see it. A lot of the litter you find could be recycled. Remember, thoughtlessly throwing things away can harm people and animals.

Look Back

Look back to page 7. Remember the pile of rubbish the children collected in one day. Take out all the things you could re-use or recycle and see what little rubbish there is left.

Compost is a soil-like material made from vegetable waste and dead plants.

Many local councils run recycling centres. They may have a composting centre, too. You can take all your vegetable and plant waste here. Once it has rotted down, compost is used as a natural fertiliser.

Have a Go!

Ask an adult to help you make your own compost heap. Find a container for kitchen scraps (not meat) and one for soft garden waste. This will reduce the amount of rubbish in your bin by about a quarter.

(A few worms from the fishing shop will help your compost to form faster.)

Making the most of rubbish

The world is so enormous that you may feel there isn't much you can do about making it a better place – but there is.

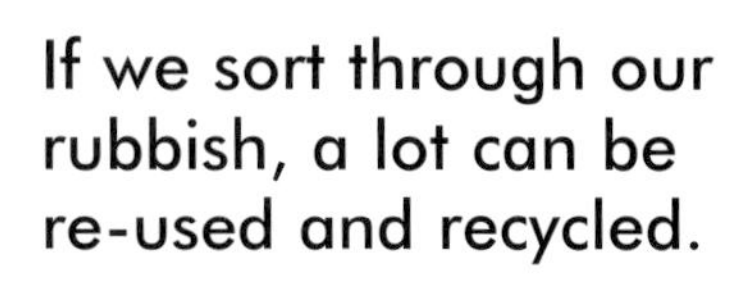

If we sort through our rubbish, a lot can be re-used and recycled.

LOOK BACK

Look back to page 12 and see how much rubbish is taken to be buried in landfill sites.

It is better if we can reduce the amount of rubbish we make in the first place. It can be fun sorting through the waste that is left to find what can be re-used or recycled. And what's left can be crushed!

Much of our waste is crushed by the refuse-collecting lorry. It is crushed again at the landfill site. But we can help crush it too.

Have a Go!

Collect some empty cardboard boxes. Pile them on top of each other. See how much space they take up. Now open them out flat and stack them. How much space do they take up now?

By recycling, re-using and especially by reducing the amount of waste we make, we *can* make a difference. We use up less of the world's precious resources, we cause less pollution by having less waste to get rid of and less energy is used as fewer new things have to be made.

So, by following the 3 Rs (reduce, re-use, recycle), we can help to make our world a better place.

More activities and facts

More things to re-use and recycle:

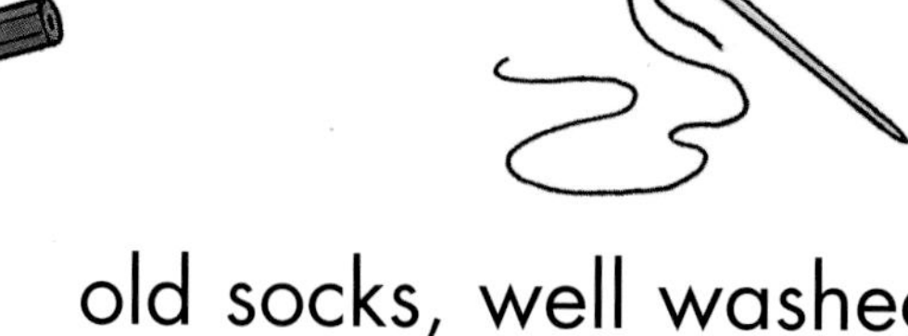

– empty plastic yogurt pots make good pencil holders or small plant pots. Whether you choose to make a plant pot or a pencil holder, you could brighten your pot by covering it in papier mâché and decorating it.

– a large cardboard box can be divided up to make your own family recycling centre. This makes collecting glass, paper, metal and material an easy task.

– old socks, well washed, make great glove puppets. (Use glue to stick on eyes, nose and a mouth from other scrap fabric.)

– empty film-canisters make excellent mini glue-pots at school. Remember to keep the lids as well so the glue doesn't dry up.

– plastic tubs can be made into crazy string holders. Decorate the outside of the tub and punch lots of holes into the sides for the string to come through.

Have a Go!

If you make a kitchen-compost heap, stick mainly to vegetable waste. Don't put meat, fish or bread, orange or lemon peel into your compost container – they don't rot well enough.

Look Back

Look back to page 21 to remind yourself how much energy can be saved by making cans from recycled aluminium rather than by making new ones.

Fascinating Facts!

Do you know what happens to our cans when we recycle them? The squashed cans are heated up until they melt. This melted metal is then used to make new metal which is rolled into long sheets. These are used to make more drink cans.

Write to local offices to ask them to donate scrap computer paper to your school. You can use this for drawing and painting on. Get them recycling too.

Useful words

aluminium: a light metal used to make many things including drink cans, cars and even aeroplanes.

chemicals: chemicals are used to help make things in factories. They are also in things like cleaning fluids that are used to clean the house.

compost: a soil-like substance made from vegetable waste and dead plants.

council: a group of people voted for by others in a local area in order to look after that area. Councils arrange for our rubbish to be collected and recycling bins to be emptied.

energy: power that gives us the ability to light things, heat and cool things and to drive things, such as machines.

incinerator: a very large oven for burning rubbish.

materials: things such as paper, glass, oil, wood, metal and fabric, from which other things are made.

ore: rock from which metals can be made.

pollute: to make the land, air or water sources dirty.

recycling centre: a place where waste materials, such as glass, paper, metal, clothes and sometimes plastic, are taken for recycling.

reduce: to use less of the earth's resources. By buying fewer goods, we reduce the need to make new things.

rot: when natural materials, such as vegetables, wood or plants, get old and break down into a soft pulp. This is what happens to compost.

tonne: a measure of weight. One tonne is the same as 1,000 kilograms.

waste: rubbish. Left over things that are no longer wanted.

Index